the modern house today

photographs Nick Dawe / text Kenneth Powell

contents

the first wave: founding fathers

Le Chateau Silver End, Essex · T S Tait · 20

Boar's Tye Road Silver End, Essex · T S Tait · 21

Silver Street Silver End, Essex · T S Tait · 23

High and Over Amersham, Buckinghamshire · Amyas Connell · 24

The White House Grayswood, Surrey · Amyas Connell · 30

Concrete House Westbury-on-Trym, Bristol · Connell & Ward · 34

High Cross House Devon · William Lescaze · 38

Hillfield Whipsnade, Buckinghamshire · Lubetkin & Tecton · 44

Holly Frindle Whipsnade, Buckinghamshire · Lubetkin & Tecton · 46

Genesta Road Plumstead, London · Berthold Lubetkin & A V Pilichowski · 48

Six Pillars Dulwich, London · Harding & Tecton · 52

Lodge Road Bromley, Kent · Samuel & Harding · 56

Levy House Chelsea, London · Gropius & Fry · 60

Cohen House Chelsea, London · Mendelsohn & Chermayeff · 61

Shrubs Wood Chalfont St Giles, Buckinghamshire · Mendelsohn & Chermayeff · 62

Shann House Rugby, Warwickshire · Serge Chermayeff · 66

classic white houses: purists and eclectics

Starlock Rye, East Sussex · Frank Scarlett · 80

St Ann's Court Chertsey, Surrey · Raymond McGrath · 82

66 Frognal Hampstead, London · Connell, Ward & Lucas · 90

Park Avenue Ruislip, Middlesex · Connell & Ward · 91

East Wall Gerrards Cross, Buckinghamshire · Elizabeth Benjamin & Godfrey Samuel · 96

Torilla Hatfield, Hertfordshire · F R S Yorke · 97

Sea Lane House Angmering-on-Sea, West Sussex · F R S Yorke & Marcel Breuer · 102

Sun House Hampstead, London · E Maxwell Fry · 106

Miramonte Coombe, Surrey · E Maxwell Fry · 108

Shipwrights Hadleigh, Essex · Wells Coates · 112

Sunspan Havant, Hampshire · Wells Coates & David Pleydell-Bouverie · 114

Pen Pits Penselwood, Somerset · P J B Harland · 116

Studio North Fordingbridge, Hampshire · Christopher Nicholson · 120

Kits Close Fawley, Buckinghamshire · Christopher Nicholson · 122

Harbour Meadow Birdham, West Sussex · Peter Moro & Richard Llewelyn Davies · 127

New Farm Great Easton, Essex · W F Crittall, Joseph & Owen Williams · 130

Landfall Poole, Dorset · Oliver Hill · 134

Cherry Hill Wentworth, Surrey · Oliver Hill · 140

Joldwynds Holmbury St Mary, Surrey	Oliver Hill	142
Hallams Lane, Chilwell, Nottinghamshire	R Myerscough-Walker	146
Condover House Llandudno, Wales	Harry Weedon	148
Salix Cambridge, Cambridgeshire	H C Hughes	152
Suntops Westcliff-on-Sea, Essex	Unknown Architect	153
Druids Hill Stoke Bishop, Bristol	Unknown Architect	154
4 – 10 Wells Rise St John's Wood, London	Francis Lorne	155
Manna Cliftonville, Kent	Unknown Architect	156
Palm Bay Avenue Cliftonville, Kent	Unknown Architect	158
Newhaven Herne Bay, Kent	Unknown Architect	159
White House Hendon, London	Evelyn Simmons	160
Stillness Bromley, Kent	Gilbert Booth	162

new suburban forms

Sunnywood Road Haywards Heath	Lubetkin & Tecton	174
Orchard Road Tewin, Hertfordshire	Mary B Crowley & Cecil G Kemp	176
The Round House Frinton-on-Sea, Essex	Oliver Hill	180
St Martin Frinton-on-Sea, Essex	Oliver Hill	182
14 – 16 Waltham Way Frinton-on-Sea, Essex	Unknown Architect	183
Dawn Frinton-on-Sea, Essex	Oliver Hill	184
Morare Frinton-on-Sea, Essex	Oliver Hill	185
Lytton Close Hampstead Garden Suburb, London	G G Winbourne	186

looking forward: the end of the modern house?

Bentley Wood Halland, East Sussex	Serge Chermayeff	196
Little Winch Chipperfield, Hertfordshire	E Maxwell Fry	200
Bessborough Road, Roehampton Vale, London	Connell Ward & Lucas	202
Ainger House Eton, Berkshire	Yorke & Breuer	206
Benson House Eton, Berkshire	Yorke & Breuer	207
The Wood House Shipbourne, Kent	Gropius & Fry	208
Carry Gate Galby, Leicestershire	Raymond McGrath	210
Brackenfell Brampton, Cumbria	J L Martin & Sadie Speight	212
Willow Road Hampstead, London	Ernö Goldfinger	214

the first wave: founding fathers

The modern house constitutes a brief, but fascinating (and, indeed, dazzling), chapter in the architectural, cultural and social history of Britain (or more particularly, of England, since modern houses were always thin on the ground in Wales, Scotland and Northern Ireland). F R S Yorke's hugely influential book, *The Modern House* appeared in 1934 "an open sesame for a new type of Continental tour" (as Maxwell Fry later described it). Yorke made available to British architects, the majority of whom had not travelled widely in Europe, let alone the United States, exemplars of the best foreign practice – 57 houses from 14 countries were illustrated and described. *The Modern House* can be seen as a potent challenge to the dominance of the Arts and Crafts (a tradition in which Yorke himself was nurtured) and as the harbinger of a modernist hegemony which extended into the 1960s. (The last edition of the book appeared, significantly, in 1962.)

When Yorke published his second book, *The Modern House in England*, in 1937, he was able to show houses built in England by leading modernists such as Gropius & Fry, Lubetkin, Chermayeff, Christopher Nicholson, Wells Coates, Connell, Ward & Lucas and Raymond McGrath, as well as more obscure practitioners, not to mention projects he had himself undertaken, either solo or in collaboration with Marcel Breuer. Geographically, the selection extended from Cornwall to Yorkshire, though there was a preponderance of examples from London and the Home Counties. In 1934, Yorke explained, "when *The Modern House* was first published, it was difficult to find material to fill the fourteen pages of the book given to English examples. Within a little more than two years, there were enough modern houses in this country to provide material for a double number of the *Architectural Review*, and now, within three years, it is possible to produce a book devoted to English houses only." The burgeoning of modern design was all the more remarkable, Yorke explained, in the light of the obstructive attitudes of local authorities driven by "aesthetic prejudice". The "Cuckfield Case" (see below) suggested, however, that a determined client could overcome the objections of local politicians.

It is significant that the foreword to *The Modern House in England* was a text by W R Lethaby in which the latter argued that "the chief obstruction to our having better houses has been the superstition that they should be built in a style". Yorke himself argued that "the struggle for a departure from revivalism, the acceptance of the machine by the artist, and the freeing of the plan... was begun in this country towards the end of the last century, by such men as Mackintosh, C F A Voysey, Edgar Wood and George Walton...".

For Yorke, and others of his generation in Britain, the relationship of modern architecture to the Arts and Crafts was rather like that of the Christian revelation to the Old Law – it fulfilled and made sense of what had gone before. It was significant, for example, that Frank Pick, an Arts and Crafts figure to the core, penned the introduction to the first English edition of Gropius's *The New Architecture and the Bauhaus* (1935), extolling the potential of "the new architecture".

For Gropius and Yorke, "modern" implied that a building reflected the modern approach to construction and responded to modern ways of living. Yorke identified Behrens' New Ways at Northampton (1926) as effectively the first truly modern house in Britain, that is a house which finally jettisoned the traditionalism inherent in the work of Mackintosh, Voysey and other designers who might, for all their commendably progressive tendencies, be broadly categorised as Arts and Crafts. Behrens was, at heart, a Classicist and it was the calm order of Classicism which underpinned the reductive, anti-ornamental work of Behrens (and his pupil Mies van der Rohe), Taut, Loos, Hoffmann and Wagner and, indeed, in a different vein, Auguste Perret, from which the Modern Movement took inspiration. After Behrens' pioneering gesture at Northampton, the work of Thomas Tait at Silver End, Amyas Connell's stunning High and Over at Amersham (1929) and the early houses by George Checkley in Cambridge pushed the new ideals into the English consciousness. The continuum of history was now, Yorke believed, in motion and modern architecture was set to become "the normal architecture of the country". This deterministic, though equally optimistic, analysis was cemented into British culture by the writings of Nikolaus Pevsner who had no doubts that "the architecture of reason and functionalism" must point the way to the future.

"Why a modern architecture?", asked J M Richards in his widely read 1940 Penguin *An Introduction to Modern Architecture*. "The principal reason why a new architecture is coming into existence", Richards wrote, echoing the practical stress of Yorke and Gropius, "is that the needs of this age are in nearly every case totally different from the needs of previous ages, and so cannot be satisfied by methods of building that belong to any age but the present." With Britain at war, attention was turning away from houses to housing – and to schools, clinics, hospitals and workplaces. The great age of the modern house was already over. The representative buildings of the immediate Post-War era were the Festival Hall, the Brynmawr Rubber Factory, the Hertfordshire schools, the Churchill Gardens estate – housing, rather than houses, was the priority.

Before the War, Yorke had freely conceded that the one-off modern houses he described and popularised were not in themselves a solution to the crisis of the cities. Rehousing the population in villas designed to the most progressive standards would merely produce "a glorified garden city". (Commercial developers who adapted the modern look for speculative housing developments had no qualms in this respect – they had no ambition to change society.) For the masses, high-density apartment blocks were the answer. Nonetheless, Yorke argued, modern houses were something more than a luxury for the affluent. The reconstruction of Britain demanded the use of modern materials and new techniques of construction: "there is no-one, apart from the client, to finance experimental buildings. And since the architect can gain real experience of new construction only in actual building work, he is most likely to find in the villa the most easily accessible unit for research." The young Hugh Casson, writing in 1938, conceded that modern houses, "stimulating as they are… merely indicate an experimental stage in culture which, before maturity, must face issues of wider and more social significance."

Flowing, open plans, large expanses of window, and flat, inhabitable roofs all facilitated a modern lifestyle. A new form of building implied new construction techniques and the use of new materials, most obviously concrete and steel. Neither material was new to inter-war England. Steel-framed and reinforced concrete construction had been commonplace for large industrial and public buildings since at least the 1900s, but usually over-clad with brick, stone or faience to produce what progressives like Yorke and Richards called a "sham". The advocates of modern architecture argued, in tones oddly reminiscent of Ruskin, that "new" materials should be used "honestly".

The passionate rhetoric about new materials notwithstanding, pure reinforced concrete or steel framed construction were, if anything, the exception rather than the rule for most British modern houses of the inter-war years. Essentially traditional or, more frequently, composite constructional techniques predominated, while prefabrication, though a particular interest of Yorke, was hardly an issue in pre-1939 Britain. William Lescaze's High Cross House, for example, though conceived as a steel-framed, concrete infill structure, was constructed in cavity wall brick, covered in render. Rendered brickwork was the dominant element in the houses at Old Church Street, Chelsea, by Gropius & Fry and Mendelsohn & Chermayeff. Lubetkin, though by conviction a structural innovator, used load-bearing brick on many occasions – the group of Tecton houses at Haywards Heath used concrete only for balconies and porches. Exposed brickwork was used unapologetically by Yorke for his development of brewery workers' houses at Stratford-on-Avon. Exposed timber and stone (used by Leslie Martin, for example, in his houses in Cumbria) further compromised the supposedly "functionalist" approach of the 1930s Modern Movement in Britain. The expressive and sculptural potential of concrete is, however, apparent in houses like Raymond McGrath's St Ann's Court, Yorke & Breuer's Sea Lane House and the pair of bungalows built by Lubetkin at Whipsnade, though again none of them supports a functionalist rationale. (Lubetkin, in particular, scorned purely functional interpretations of his work.)

The critic Alan Powers has argued convincingly against a purely functionalist interpretation of the modern house, linking it with the surrealist movement and its pursuit of the shockingly novel and bizarre. The imagery of the modern house, it could be said, counted for more than the reality. Its most potent image today is that of the "white box", – cool, clean and exact. In reality, the compromises and failings of the construction process made many houses less precise in finish and detail than their architects would have wished, while colour was widely used externally. Blue was applied, for example, at High Cross House, while Connell's White House (New Farm) at Grayswood was painted "sugar almond pink" and McGrath's St Ann's Court "a pale pinkish grey".

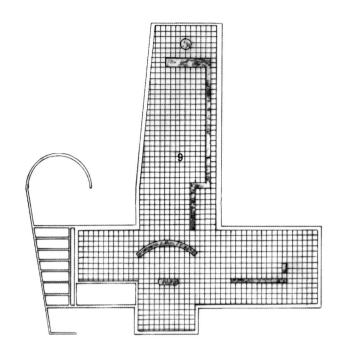

Roof Plan

Lubetkin & Tecton
Hillfield
Whipsnade
Buckinghamshire
1933-36

1 Bathroom
2 Bedroom
3 Hall
4 Dining room
5 Living room
6 Kitchen
7 Loggia
8 Terrace
9 Roof terrace

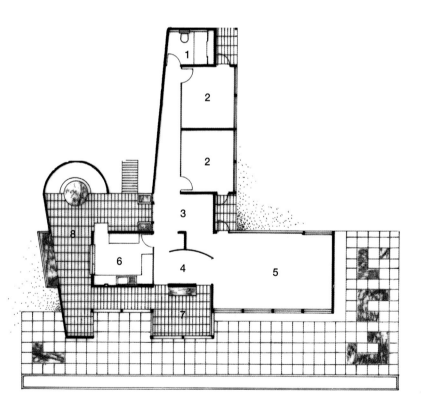

Ground Floor Plan

0 1   10

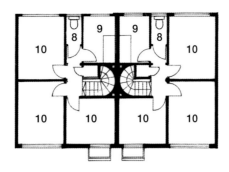

Second Floor Plan

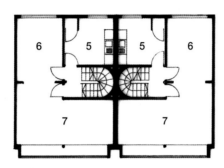

First Floor Plan

Lubetkin & Pilichowski

Genesta Road

Plumstead

London

1933-34

1 Yard

2 Garage

3 Entrance

4 Hall

5 Kitchen

6 Dining room

7 Living room

8 WC

9 Bathroom

10 Bedroom

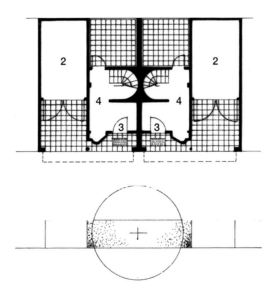

Ground Floor Plan

0 1   10

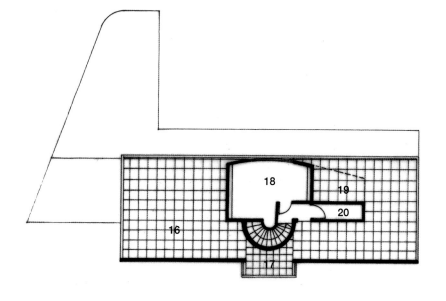

Roof Plan

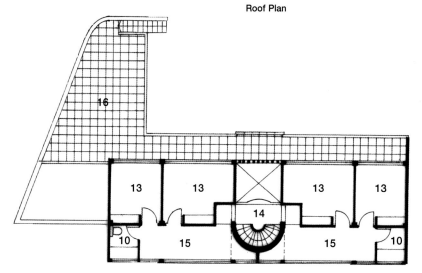

First Floor Plan

Harding & Tecton
Six Pillars
Dulwich
London
1934-35

1 Living room
2 Hall
3 Dining room
4 Maid's room
5 WC
6 Entrance
7 Pantry
8 Kitchen
9 Maid's bedroom
10 Bathroom
11 Coal store
12 Garage
13 Bedroom
14 Gallery
15 Corridor
16 Terrace
17 Balcony
18 Study
19 Shelter
20 Box room

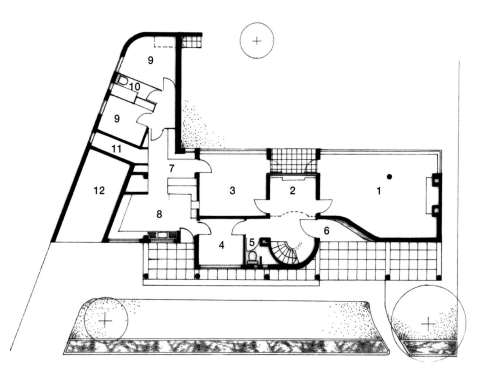

Ground Floor Plan

0 1   10

Mendelsohn & Chermayeff
Cohen House
Chelsea
London
1935-36

1	Hall
2	Service
3	Kitchen
4	Staff room
5	Garage
6	Squash court
7	Dining room
8	Library
9	Drawing room
10	Cloak room
11	Landing
12	Maid
13	Man's room
14	Maids bathroom
15	Bedroom
16	Bathroom
17	Lobby
18	Cupboard
19	Study
20	Dressing room
21	WC
22	Balcony
23	Terrace

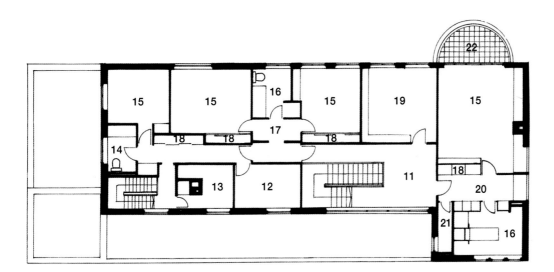

First Floor Plan

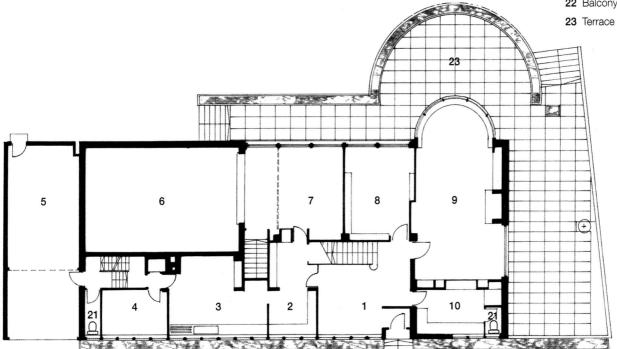

Ground Floor Plan

0   1   10

Gropius & Fry
Levy House
Chelsea
London
1935-36

1 Maid's quarters

2 Bathroom

3 Cupboard

4 Night nursery

5 Secretary

6 Day nursery

7 Laundry

8 Study

9 Bedroom

10 Terrace

11 Garage

12 Washing yard

13 Butler

14 WC

15 Playroom

16 Living room

17 Dining room

18 Pantry

19 Kitchen

20 Staff

21 Covered terrace

22 Open terrace

23 Loggia

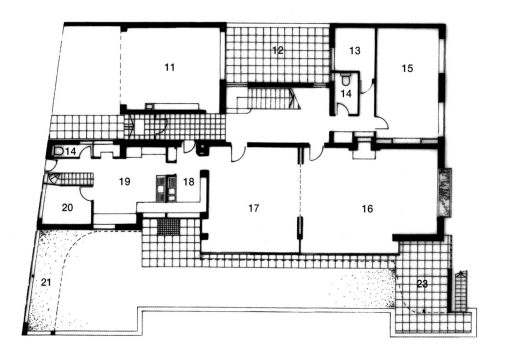

Ground Floor Plan

0   1   10

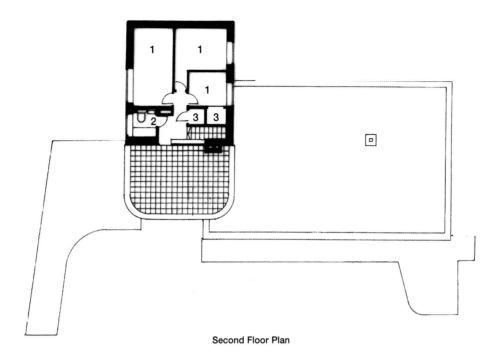

Second Floor Plan

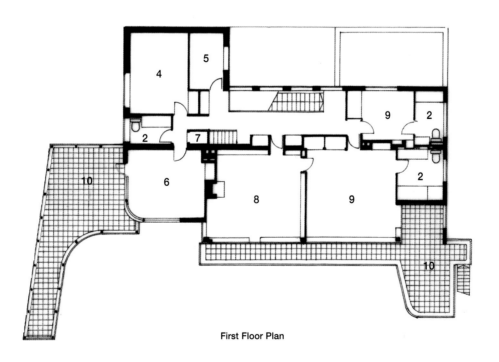

First Floor Plan

Le Chateau   T S Tait   1927
Silver End, Essex

Le Chateau at Silver End was designed by Tait – probably the only house there in which he was personally involved – for Dan Crittall, a member of the window manufacturing family which founded the modernist settlement.

Boar's Tye Road   T S Tait   1927
Silver End, Essex

the first wave: founding fathers

Silver Street   T S Tait   1927
Silver End, Essex

The new village at Silver End was planned by the Crittall company to have "all the advantages of a town, without the drawbacks of such places". Development began in 1925, with Thomas Tait as lead architect – his assistant Frederick MacManus carried out most of the design work. Behrens' recently completed New Ways at Northampton, usually credited as the first truly modern house in Britain, was a clear inspiration.

High and Over   Amyas Connell   1929-31
Amersham, Buckinghamshire

High and Over at Amersham marked the stunning debut of Amyas Connell on the British architectural scene
– the house remains one of the most dynamic and uncompromising products of the first wave of the Modern
Movement in England. The client was Bernard Ashmole, Professor of Archaeology at London University,
whom Connell had met at the British School in Rome.

the first wave: founding fathers

Ashmole's objectives in commissioning Connell were "to take utmost advantage of the scanty English sunshine; to enjoy to the full the magnificent views across and up the valley of the Misbourne; and to conform to the immediate contours." The Y-plan was intended as a sun-trap facing south and west. A nursery was located on the roof.

To the north and east, the house shows a protective and private facade. Although now divided into two dwellings – the plan facilitates subdivision – it retains a number of original internal features.

The White House   Amyas Connell   1931-32
Grayswood, Surrey

Connell, Ward & Lucas's New Farm has now been re-named The White House. It was originally, however,
painted pink. The house is a classic expression of the ideals of the Modern Movement, with its virtuoso use
of natural light and quest for sunshine. The garden is an important element of the total ensemble.

The plan is typically dynamic, with the principal rooms canting out to take maximum advantage of natural light from the south and the entrance and servants' wing presenting a more private and protective face to the north.

Concrete House   Connell & Ward   1934-35
Westbury-on-Trym, Bristol

The matter-of-fact name given to this important house by Connell & Ward does not detract from its quality. Externally and internally, the house is uncommonly intact.

On the rare occasions when the Concrete House is open to the public, queues have been known to extend along the street. The house has also featured in television programmes.

The use of colour at High Cross House is according to the original designs, as restored by architect John Winter. The house is one of a small number of British buildings realised between the wars by an American architect – Swiss-born Lescaze, better known for his skyscrapers, had previously designed the school in Philadelphia at which Dartington's headmaster, William Curry, had taught.

High Cross House is one of only two modern houses in Britain regularly open to the public – the surrounding estate contains a number of other pioneering modern buildings. Modern architecture was seen as the natural ally of progressive educational theories.

Lubetkin's two "dachas" at Whipsnade, on the Bedfordshire/Buckinghamshire border, originally known as Bungalows A and B, were highly personal works, one designed for a friend, the other as the architect's own weekend retreat. They take advantage of splendid views over open countryside and typify the enthusiastic modernist response to the natural landscape. Both houses have been very well restored in recent years – "Holly Frindle" from a state of advanced decay.

Genesta Road   Berthold Lubetkin   1933-34
Plumstead, London   & A V Pilichowski

The classic image of the modern house is of a white pavilion, freestanding in a green landscape. The ambition of the Modern Movement was, however, to recast the cities. At Genesta Road, Plumstead, in the depths of Victorian South London, Lubetkin grappled with the issue of context. His group of houses fills a gap in a mundane nineteenth century terrace (previously an orchard).

Lubetkin's Genesta Road houses adopt the classic Georgian town house format of principal rooms at first floor level, with space for cars below.

the first wave: founding fathers

Six Pillars is an example of the work of the Tecton partnership, in this case led by Valentine Harding. Tecton was formed by Lubetkin in 1932 and continued in existence, with a changing cast of members (Harding quit in 1936) until 1948.

The house opens up to the garden front to take advantage of views over extensive grounds. The servants' wing, still a necessary feature of middle-class houses, is distinctly subsidiary, with no views out – the democratic ideals of the Modern Movement often had to compromise with the social conventions of the time.

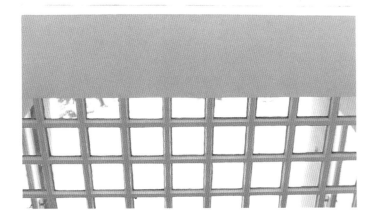

Lodge Road   Samuel & Harding   1934-35
Bromley, Kent

The original setting of this house by Samuel & Harding of Tecton has been somewhat compromised by later development, but enough survives to indicate the close relationship between house and garden.

| Levy House | Gropius & Fry | 1935-36 |
| Chelsea, London | | |

At Old Church Street, Chelsea, two of the giants of the Modern Movement, Gropius and Mendelsohn, both in transit to the United States, worked at close proximity, though the two houses, built for emigre cousins (Benn Levy and Dennis Cohen) are very different. Gropius's Levy House suffers from unsympathetic recladding. The new conservatory at the Cohen House is the work of Norman Foster.

the first wave: founding fathers

Cohen House   Mendelsohn & Chermayeff   1935-36
Chelsea, London

In both cases, the distinguished foreign architects had to collaborate with British practitioners – Gropius
with Maxwell Fry, Mendelsohn with Serge Chermayeff (born in Russia, but schooled in Britain).

Shrubs Wood   Mendelsohn & Chermayeff   1933-35
Chalfont St Giles, Buckinghamshire

     the first wave: founding fathers

In this house of 1933-35, Mendelsohn & Chermayeff adopted a version of the plan seen at their greatest collaborative work, the Bexhill Pavilion. A long wing contains the main living room at ground level, with nursery and guest accommodation above. As usual, the main elevation features large (in this case, sliding) windows taking advantage of light from the south-west.

the first wave: founding fathers

The north facade features smaller openings illuminating a corridor, cloakrooms and maid's quarters. Garage and service space is at basement level. A broad terrace provides a good vantage point for extensive views out. The glazed staircase is a key feature.

Shann House   Serge Chermayeff   1933-34
Rugby, Warwickshire

In this relatively modest house, Chermayeff, working on his own, demonstrated his grasp of planning and ability to create highly enjoyable spaces which open up to the light and fresh air.

classic white houses: purists and eclectics

The comic, but slightly sinister, figure of Dr Silenus in Evelyn Waugh's *Decline and Fall* (1928) could be seen as a caricature of Peter Behrens or, perhaps, Walter Gropius. It was equally a premonition of the influx of foreign modernists who came to Britain, often en route for the United States, from the early 30s onward. Berthold Lubetkin arrived in 1931 – from Russia, via Warsaw and Paris. Erich Mendelsohn, best known for his fine department stores in Germany, reached London in 1933, Walter Gropius and Ernö Goldfinger a year later, and Marcel Breuer in 1935. Gropius and Breuer departed for Harvard in 1937. Mendelsohn went to the United States in 1939. Both Lubetkin and Goldfinger (born in 1901 and 1902 respectively) remained in London and built extensively, making a lasting impact on the British architectural scene. Connell, Ward & Lucas, like Wells Coates, a Canadian and instrumental in the establishment of the MARS group, had their origins in the British Empire.

The emigres found a Britain where modern architecture was still regarded as a novelty, even a curiosity. Amongst the few developments which suggested it had any social relevance was the flat-roofed model village at Silver End, near Braintree in Essex, built by Francis Crittall, the window manufacturer, from 1925 onwards. Most of the houses were designed by Frederick MacManus, though Le Chateau (for one of Crittall's sons) was done by Thomas Tait, then seen, in British terms, as a fairly extreme modernist (though it was Tait who designed the Daily Telegraph's Fleet Street headquarters in opulently Classical manner).

The work of Connell, Ward & Lucas was soon to shift the debate on modernism to a higher plane. Connell (1901-80) had come to London from New Zealand in 1924, with his friend Basil Ward (1902-76). Both studied at the Bartlett and both won scholarships to Rome, where Connell met the archaeologist Bernard Ashmole, his client for High and Over at Amersham (built 1929-31). This large and outstanding house responded powerfully to the remarkable Chilterns setting, with three wings radiating out from a central, double-height hall (it has since been sub divided). Connell, Ward & Lucas – the third partner was Colin Lucas (1906-88) – later built a number of smaller houses in the vicinity of High and Over. New Farm (now The White House) at Grayswood, Surrey, followed soon after. Connell, Ward & Lucas's work was notable for its uncompromising, geometric and (some critics alleged) mechanistic look.

William Lescaze, Swiss-born but working in the United States from 1920 onwards, was best known for the Philadelphia Saving Fund tower. The commission to design High Cross House and other buildings at Dartington came about through the progressive headmaster William Curry – since Dartington was a new sort of school, it was logical that it should embrace a new school of design.

Once established in England, Berthold Lubetkin quickly founded a practice, Tecton, with Godfrey Samuel and a group of fellow students from the Architectural Association as partners. His ambitions were to build on a scale and in tune with a radically progressive view of society. Tecton was as much a research establishment as an architectural practice and it was in this light that its domestic commissions were seen – after the Second World War, the firm built large amounts of social housing. Lubetkin designed Six Pillars at Dulwich (1934-35) with his young partner Valentine Harding. In this house and in the group of houses at Plumstead, Lubetkin demonstrated his ability to marry structural and compositional innovation with a nod to the English urban tradition. The two bungalows or "dachas" at Whipsnade (1936) have a strong personality and relationship to their context which reflects their history. Bungalow A was Lubetkin's own weekend retreat and reflects his romantic and sensual philosophy of life – far removed from the functionalism of the MARS group. As objects in the landscape, these houses are as enjoyable as the follies and pavilions of the Georgian age.

The Cohen and Levy houses in Old Church Street designed by Gropius & Fry and Mendelsohn & Chermayeff – the Levy house has been unsympathetically reclad against the weather – were both sizeable, designed for families with servants. They can be seen as part of a tradition of innovative domestic design in Chelsea extending back into the nineteenth century and are significant as a remarkably well-mannered modernist response to the street – as if the time for radical gestures had already passed.

At Shrub's Wood, for an American client, Mendelsohn & Chermayeff designed an equally serene response to a semi-rural landscape. The site was a cherry orchard, with extensive views over wooded Buckinghamshire country. The most dramatic feature was the glazed semi-circular staircase rising through the double-height hall, an echo of the stair at the Bexhill Pavilion.

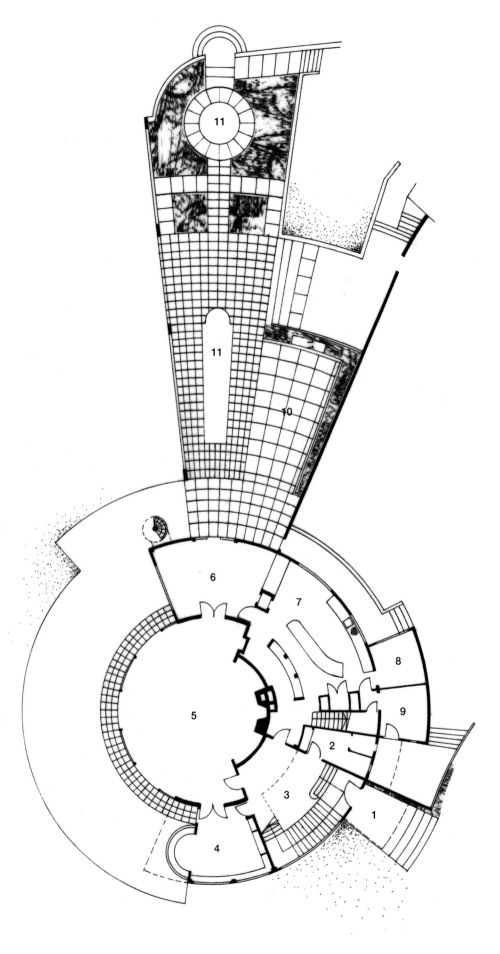

Ground Floor Plan

0 1   10

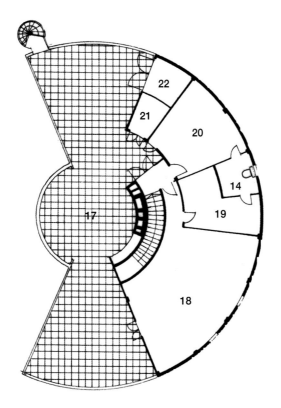

Second Floor Plan

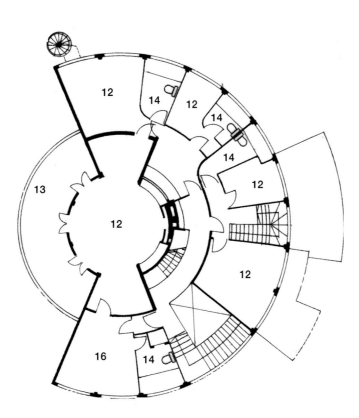

First Floor Plan

Raymond McGrath
St Ann's Court
Chertsey
Surrey
1936-37

1 Entrance
2 Cloaks
3 Hall
4 Study
5 Living room
6 Dining room
7 Kitchen
8 Breakfast room
9 Utility room
10 Winter garden
11 Pool
12 Bedroom
13 Balcony
14 Bathroom
15 Ironing room
16 Dressing room
17 Terrace
18 Billiard's room
19 Box room
20 Studio
21 Store
22 Tanks

F R S Yorke
Torilla
Hatfield
Hertfordshire
1934-35

1   Living room
2   Dining room
3   Larder
4   Pantry
5   Kitchen
6   Bedroom
7   Bathroom
8   Landing
9   Garage
10 Terrace

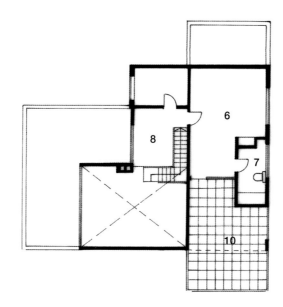

First Floor Plan

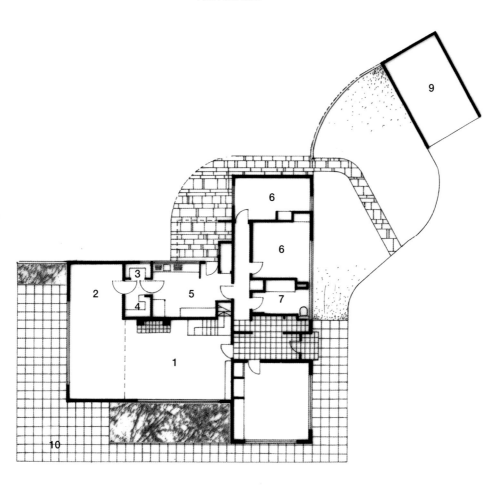

Ground Floor Plan

0   1   10

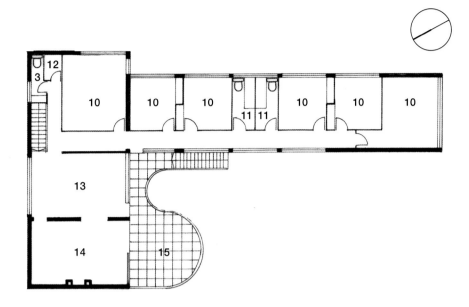

F R S Yorke
& Marcel Breuer
Sea Lane House
Angmering-on-Sea
West Sussex
1937

1 Entrance
2 Hall
3 WC
4 Garage
5 Kitchen
6 Larder
7 Store
8 Fuel store
9 Maid's room
10 Bedroom
11 Bathroom
12 Linen room
13 Dining room
14 Living room
15 Terrace

First Floor Plan

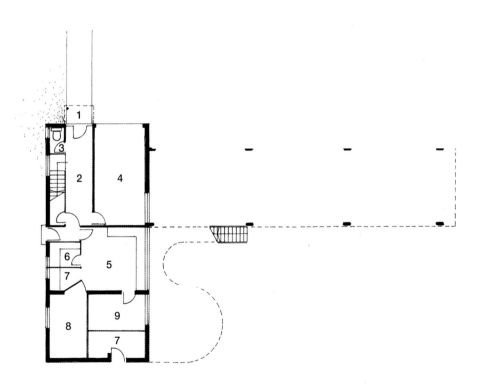

Ground Floor Plan

0   1   10

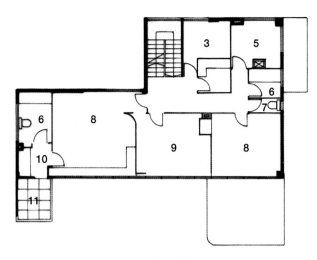

Second Floor Plan

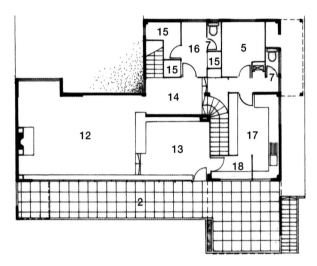

First Floor Plan

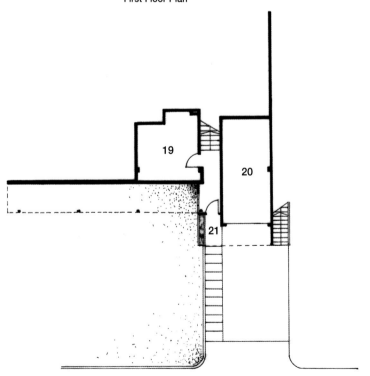

Ground Floor Plan

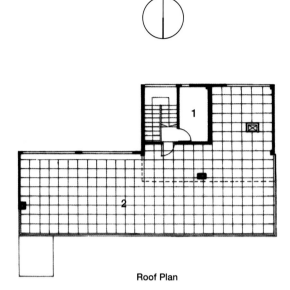

Roof Plan

E Maxwell Fry
Sun House
Hampstead
London
1935-36

1 Tanks
2 Sewing room
3 Dark room
4 Maid's room
5 Bathroom
6 Day nursery
7 WC
8 Bedroom
9 Dressing room
10 Lobby
11 Balcony
12 living
13 Dining
14 Hall
15 Cupboard/store
16 Cloaks
17 Kitchen
18 Servery
19 Heating plant room
20 Garage
21 Entrance

0 1   10

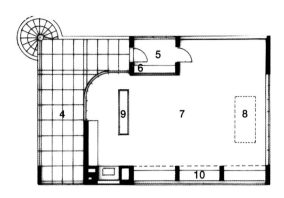

First Floor Plan

Christopher Nicholson
Studio North
Fordingbridge
Hampshire
1933-34

1 Picture store
2 WC
3 Trap above
4 Terrace
5 Lobby
6 Cupboard
7 Studio
8 Skylight above
9 Floor trap
10 Window seats

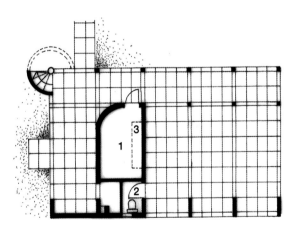

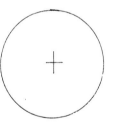

Ground Floor Plan

0 1   10

Peter Moro
& Richard Llewelyn Davies
Harbour Meadow
Birdham
West Sussex
1941

1 Entrance Hall
2 Dining room
3 Lounge room
4 drawing room
5 Sun terrace
6 Pantry
7 Cloakroom
8 Larder
9 WC
10 Nursery
11 Kitchen
12 Store
13 Maid
14 Laundry/Maid's room
15 Landing
16 Owner's bedroom
17 Dressing room
18 Cupboard
19 Owner's room
20 Sun loggia
21 Stair to roof
22 Balcony
23 Bathroom
24 Guest bedroom
25 Children's bedroom
26 Nurse
27 House keeper

First Floor Plan

Ground Floor Plan

0   1   10

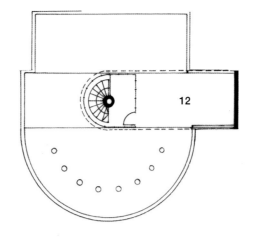

Roof Plan

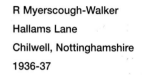

R Myerscough-Walker
Hallams Lane
Chilwell, Nottinghamshire
1936-37

1 Lobby
2 WC
3 Hall
4 Dining space
5 Living space
6 Kitchen
7 Garage
8 Maid's room
9 Dressing room
10 Bedroom
11 Bathroom
12 Covered terrace

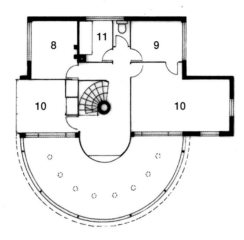

First Floor Plan

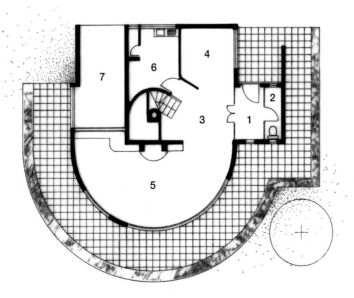

Ground Floor Plan

0 1   10

Starlock   Frank Scarlett   1930
Rye, East Sussex

The relatively unknown Frank Scarlett of Scarlett & Ashworth was an active designer in the "modernistic" mould – the symmetrical plan and formality of this house set it apart from the deliberate asymmetry of the purists. The small pavilion was built to house the chauffeur employed by the clients, Colonel and Mrs Templar.

St Ann's Court
Chertsey, Surrey

Raymond McGrath

1936-37

classic white houses: purists and eclectics

Raymond McGrath's St Ann's Court is one of the largest and most ambitious of the modern houses of the 1930s, built for Gerald Schlesinger and his partner, the landscape designer Christopher Tunnard (who laid out the gardens). The house successfully utilises the circular plan explored by a number of architects at the time (for example, Myerscough-Walker at Chilwell, Nottingham)

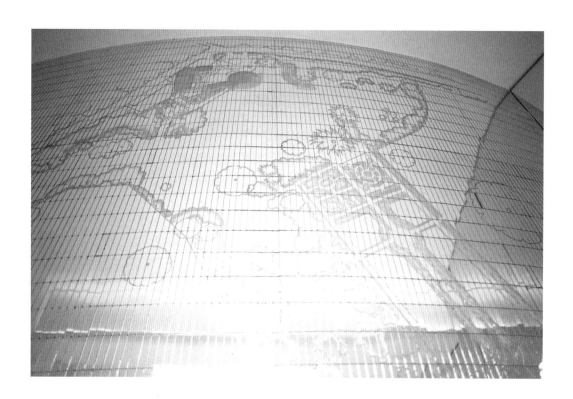

classic white houses: purists and eclectics

McGrath (1903-77) was Australian by birth and was launched on the British architectural scene by Mansfield Forbes, his client for the refit of Forbes' house Finella in Cambridge.

The recent restoration of St Ann's Court by Munkenbeck & Marshall has removed later "Deco" accretions and reinstated the house's credentials as an innovative and forward-looking modernist work. The shuttered finish of the concrete, for example, anticipates a taste developed by the Brutalists of the 1960s.

Though imposing, the house has relatively few rooms. The staircase is the heart of the building, a glamorous concept enhanced by the skilful use of mirrors – McGrath's standard work on *Glass in Architecture and Decoration* appeared in 1937.

66 Frognal   Connell, Ward & Lucas   1936-38

Hampstead, London

Connell, Ward & Lucas's Frognal house is one of a number of modern houses built during the 1930s in Hampstead – in this case, as elsewhere, against opposition from more conservative local residents.

Park Avenue   Connell & Ward   1933-35
Ruislip, Middlesex

The three houses by Connell & Ward at Park Avenue, Ruislip (1933-35), were designed for a local developer and reflect the willingness of leading-edge modernists to work with spec-builders. (In practice, such relationships rarely turned out to be either amicable or lasting.)

classic white houses: purists and eclectics

The houses at Park Avenue were designed as a carefully composed group, in the tradition of modernist developments, for example, in the suburbs of Paris. They have suffered in recent years from a series of alterations – for example, the conversion of a garage to a living room and the infilling of an open roof terrace.

| East Wall | Elizabeth Benjamin | 1936 |
| Gerrards Cross, Buckinghamshire | & Godfrey Samuel | |

Designed by Elizabeth Benjamin in association with Godfrey Samuel of Tecton, the house was known by the architects as "the George and Dragon House". (The name originated with the idea of the white concrete frame of the house as a knight bestriding a bare brick wall – the dragon.) It was built for a paint manufacturer, Arnold Osorio, and was the major work of this woman architect.

classic white houses: purists and eclectics

Torilla   F R S Yorke   1934-35
Hatfield, Hertfordshire

Torilla was the first important work of F R S Yorke and its construction overlapped with the publication of the first edition of *The Modern House* (1934). Built of reinforced concrete, it was based on close study of contemporary European examples, though it is not particularly Corbusian – the large central hall was, Yorke explained, a memory of the Middle Ages, reflecting his own Arts and Crafts roots.

classic white houses: purists and eclectics

Slightly extended in 1936 by Yorke and Marcel Breuer, Torilla is now a model of sensitive restoration and repair, carried out by architect John Winter for an enthusiastic owner. In the 1980s, however, the house faced possible demolition and its future was only assured after a public inquiry in 1993 led to a categorical refusal of consent to demolish.

Sea Lane House   F R S Yorke & Marcel Breuer   1937
Angmering-on-sea, West Sussex

     classic white houses: purists and eclectics

Sea Lane House at Angmering, Sussex, was the product of the brief partnership (1935-37) between Yorke and the Hungarian-born Marcel Breuer, who subsequently followed Gropius to Harvard. In fact, it is entirely the work of Breuer – his only surviving building in Britain. By elevating the house on piloti, Breuer provided views over the top of neighbouring houses. (He proposed a third storey, but this was vetoed by local planners.) As built, the house is a daring, even subversive exercise in the context of conservative local attitudes.

Sea Lane House was built of brick, with the projecting bedroom wing supported on a reinforced concrete slab – the garden extends beneath it. The boldly projecting sun terrace, opening off the living room, reflects Breuer's taste for strongly sculptural effects in his work.

One of a number of controversial Hampstead houses of the 30s, Sun House, with its strong Miesian influence, exemplifies the work of Max Fry, a modernist even before his two year collaboration with Gropius. Fry (1899-1987) was to remain an influential figure on the world scene during the Post-War period – he assisted Corbusier with Chandigarh in the early 50s.

| Miramonte | E Maxwell Fry | 1936-37 |
| Coombe, Surrey | | |

Though currently in a poor condition, Miramonte is perhaps Fry's finest house and reflects the continuing influence of Mies van der Rohe (and particularly the highly disciplined Tugendhat House) on this leading British modernist. With its swimming pool and sun terrace, the house underlines the modernist preoccupation with healthy living.

Shipwrights   Wells Coates   1936
Hadleigh, Essex

Shipwrights was commissioned by the Ekco radio company, for which Wells Coates worked extensively. It
was intended as a weekend retreat for company executives

The idea of the Sunspan house was born with the model house which Coates designed for the Ideal Home Exhibition. Large numbers of such houses were projected, but few were realised – this is the grandest example and retains many period details.

Pen Pits   P J B Harland   1935

Penselwood, Somerset

Built for composer Arthur Bliss, Pen Pits is the major work of P J B Harland (1900-73). A music room was provided on a site amongst trees some distance from the house. Harland went on to design a house for Gerald Finzi.

Studio North   Christopher Nicholson   1933-34
Fordingbridge, Hampshire

Augustus John, a senior, but far from avant-garde, figure on the British art scene, went to Christopher (Kit) Nicholson, son of his fellow painter William Nicholson, for his new studio at Fordingbridge, built in 1933-34. This was Nicholson's first major commission and marked his conversion to serious modernism. The studio was originally a single large room raised on piloti – the ground floor was filled in c.1970 when the building was converted for use as a house.

Kits Close   Christopher Nicholson   1936-37
Fawley, Buckinghamshire

Kits Close is the major work of Christopher Nicholson, who died tragically in a gliding accident in 1948. It was designed for a Dr Crowe and was built (in 1936-37) only after a prolonged planning battle – a condition of consent was that the house be screened from view by a row of trees.

The house, well integrated with its splendid garden, is a dynamic product of Nicholson's growing practice (in which Hugh Casson was an assistant), embracing the open air, sunlight and views.

| Harbour Meadow | Peter Moro | 1941 |
| Birdham, West Sussex | & Richard Llewelyn Davies | |

Harbour Meadow is sometimes described as the last modern house – it was completed, by special licence, after the outbreak of hostilities. Although Moro was a refugee from Hitler's Europe, he encountered suspicion from locals – it was rumoured (incredibly) that the plan of the house was engineered as a marker for German bombers. Later interned for a time, Moro went on to design the interior of the Royal Festival Hall and a number of major theatres.

New Farm   W F Crittall,   1934
Great Easton, Essex   Joseph & Owen Williams

New Farm was built for a member of the Crittall family, W F ("Pink") Crittall – hence the pink hue of its exterior? The Crittalls were the founders of Silver End (which is some 15 miles distant) and their products were used extensively in this large, symmetrical house. The design was a collaboration between the commercial practice of Messrs Joseph with engineer Sir Owen Williams. New Farm is notable for the quality of its finely crafted interiors, which are by no means conventionally modern in character.

Landfall   Oliver Hill   1936-38
Poole, Dorset

Landfall was the last of Oliver Hill's modern houses of the 1930s and was completed on the eve of the Second World War. The garden front is a magnificent composition, lean and elegant, with a first floor balcony accessed via a curvaceous staircase.

The client was a film maker and the hall was fitted up for occasional use as a cinema. Landfall reflects Hill's absolute, but undogmatic, command of the modernist language, which he used with a fluency and apparent conviction which might seem at odds with his ingrained traditionalism.

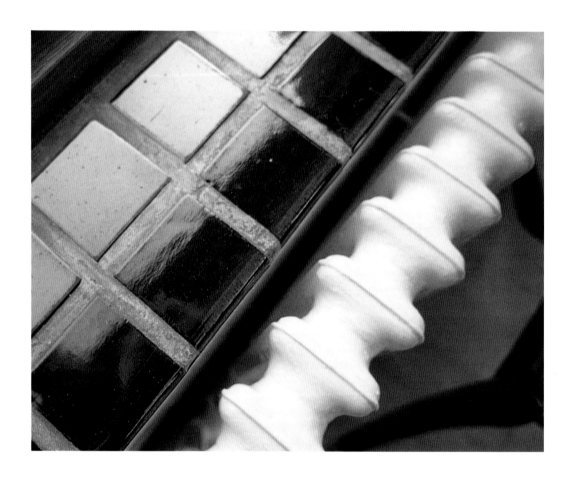

classic white houses: purists and eclectics

Cherry Hill   Oliver Hill   1933-35
Wentworth, Surrey

Hill's Cherry Hill (originally Holthanger) at Wentworth (1933-35) follows the established modernist device of a highly glazed facade to the garden, sun and views, with a more enclose and private entrance/ service frontage to the road. The full height glazed staircase is a bold gesture towards the European Modern Movement.

Joldwynds   Oliver Hill   1932-34

Holmbury St Mary, Surrey

Joldwynds replaced an important house by Philip Webb (who was, ironically, increasingly seen during the 1930s as a pioneer of modernism). The new house was located slightly away from the old site – the stables and garden buildings were retained.

Completed in 1933, Joldwynds was Oliver Hill's first exercise in the modern style – its modernistic, rather Deco appearance would not have been approved of by hardliners. The entrance front is a highly formal composition, focussing on the glazed stair. The garden front overlooks a series of stepped terraces.

Hallams Lane   R Myerscough-Walker   1936-37

Chilwell, Nottinghamshire

Raymond Myerscough-Walker was better known as a professional (and brilliant) perspectivist than as an architect – he worked for Giles Scott, Charles Holden and Edward Maufe, but was a modernist by conviction. His only house, near Nottingham, is a virtuoso work, intended to be circular in plan – it was never completed.

Condover House   Harry Weedon   1936
Llandudno, Wales

This extraordinary house at Llandudno, on the North Wales coast, is a rare domestic work by Harry Weedon (1888-1970), best known as the architect of a large number of Odeon cinemas. It draws freely and with wit on a number of Modern Movement motifs, yet remains unashamedly modernistic in character. The use of natural stone terracing successfully ties the house to the seashore.

Salix   H C Hughes   1934
Cambridge, Cambridgeshire

Modern architecture arrived in Cambridge with Raymond McGrath's 1927-29 reconstruction of Finella in Queen's Road for the don Mansfield Forbes. A series of new houses followed, a number of them designed by Henry C Hughes, of which Salix , formerly known as "Brandon Hill", is probably the finest. Cambridge-based Hughes scored a major breakthrough by winning a commission for a new building at Peterhouse.

Suntops   Unknown Architect   Unknown Date
Westcliff-on-Sea, Essex

Between the end of the First World War and the start of the Second some four million houses were built in the UK. Of these, approximately 2000 were flat roofed, and of that number about 1000 were architect designed. Throughout the country we can find these often one-off, and in their own way unique houses, built on a speculative basis by local builders or unknown architects hoping to cash in on this new desire for modern living.

Druids Hill   Unknown Architect   Late 1930s
Stoke Bishop, Bristol

       classic white houses: purists and eclectics

4 – 10 Wells Rise   Francis Lorne   1934
St John's Wood, London

Manna   Unknown Architect   Unknown Date
Cliftonville, Kent

classic white houses: purists and eclectics

Houses with a flat roof, built in the 1930s are often generically referred to as Art Deco, particularly when they are white. Although there are a huge number of houses with detailing and features reminiscent of the the term – as suburbs throughout the country show – very few true Art Deco houses exist in the UK. Art Deco is more closely associated with cinemas, lidos and factories built for American clients, such as those for Hoover and Firestone in London. However, what these various isolated domestic examples show is that they do in fact resemble a tendency towards Art Deco with their use of colour, tiling and detailing.

Newhaven   Unknown Architect   Unknown Date
Herne Bay, Kent

White House   Evelyn Simmons   1936
Hendon, London

White House epitomises the transformation of modern into modernistic. This distinctive (and immaculately maintained) suburban house by Evelyn Simmons draws freely on the motifs of the modern house, but overlays them with strong infusions of Art Deco

Stillness   Gilbert Booth   1934
Bromley, Kent

Another house which is modernistic, rather than mainstream modern, though powerfully composed and well detailed by the otherwise obscure Gilbert Booth. Finely fitted interiors make this perhaps the most complete and impressive example of its style in Britain.

new suburban forms

One symptom of the advance of the "new architecture" which had struck roots in Britain by the mid 30s was its adoption by architects who were not considered 'modern'. Messrs Joseph, who designed New Farm for W F Crittall were firmly "middle of the road" – one of their best known jobs was the streamlined Shell Mex House on the Embankment. No mainstream modern would have sanctioned the strict symmetry of the designs and the carefully crafted interior of the house – the setting for collections of pictures and porcelain – suggests a traditional concern for comfort and elegance.

Modern architects of the MARS persuasion had a clear idea of which of their fellow practitioners were in their camp and which were firmly outside. The "modernistic" approach of many commercial practices and of house developers cashing in on the vogue for modern architecture was despised by hardcore modernists – the idea that modern architecture was just a style, to be applied as an alternative to neo-Georgian or Tudor, was heresy to true believers. In most cases, the boundary between "modern" and "modernistic" is clearly drawn.

The career and works of Oliver Hill, however, challenge exact analysis. Hill (1887-1968) was of an earlier generation to that of Lubetkin, Connell, Fry and other leading edge designers. His early work was strongly influenced by Lutyens and he worked happily in a wide range of styles, ending up as an Arts and Crafts revivalist at Daneway in Gloucestershire. With the Modern Movement in full flow, however, Hill – already influenced by Scandinavian modernism – embraced it energetically and worked fluently in a modern manner. An outstanding house by Philip Webb (sometimes counted amongst the "pioneers of modern design") was demolished for Hill's Joldwynds (1932-34). At Joldwynds and at Holthanger (Cherry Hill) at Wentworth, Hill steered a tight course between the strictly modern and the moderne Art Deco style, with brilliant results – in aesthetic terms, at least: these were stylish, even glamorous, houses, though there were soon problems with both the roofing and external render of Joldwynds, which had to be corrected at Hill's expense. At Landfall, Poole, completed on the eve of the War, Hill excised the showy "Deco" elements from his style to produce a straightforward and unshowy modern design which triumphs through sure proportion and excellent detailing. An ominous portent was the provision of a built-in air-raid shelter.

The clients for modern houses were even more variegated than their architects. Landfall was built for a filmmaker. Artistic and creative types were natural enthusiasts for modern design (though Max Fry's client at Miramonte was described by David Dean as "successively furrier, off-licensee and real estate wizard". Pen Pits at Penselwood, Somerset, was designed by P J B Harland for composer Arthur Bliss (who lived long enough to become a knighted, reactionary Master of the Queen's Musick). Harland's subsequent career lay in the field of hospital design. The studio house at Fryern Court, Fordingbridge, Hampshire, was designed for painter Augustus John – who was not a particularly progressive artist – by Christopher (Kit) Nicholson, son of the painter William Nicholson and brother of Ben Nicholson (who autographed the cloakroom door). On a far grander scale was the fortuitously named Kit's Close at Fawley, Buckinghamshire – perhaps the major work of an architect whose career (which embraced the revamping of Lutyens' Monkton for the eccentric Edward James) ended tragically in a gliding accident in 1948. Progressive political attitudes were often the corollary of a taste for modern design. Modernism seemed equally to accord with ideas of sexual freedom. Wells Coates' Shipwrights was used for hedonistic weekends by executives of the Ekco company (for which Coates designed radios). Harding & Tecton's Six Pillars was allegedly built for a classic *menage a trois*. A homosexual couple were Raymond McGrath's clients for St Ann's Court (originally St Ann's Hill).

McGrath (1903-77), whose later career took him to prominence in Ireland, was an Australian who studied at Cambridge, where he was taken up by the modern-minded don Mansfield Forbes. In 1934, he published *Twentieth Century Houses*, an incisive study of the practical aspects of domestic design. St Ann's Hill allowed McGrath to bring his ideas to reality on the basis of a generous budget. The house, built of reinforced concrete, takes the form of a semi-circle, with the living room and, above, the principal bedroom, opening on to an external balcony, as its pivot. The double height staircase hall is the most impressive space, with a skilful use of mirrors. In several respects, apart from its scale, the house stands apart from others of the period. To anybody raised on late twentieth century architecture, its bold, confident forms seem to pre-empt those of Richard Meier, while its shuttered concrete finish looks forward to the New Brutalism of the 1950s and 60s. Finally, McGrath responds strongly to the Georgian landscape – an eighteenth century house was demolished for to make way for McGrath's – which was reconfigured by Christopher Tunnard. One of the relatively few British houses of the period with clearly international quality, St Ann's Court (as it is now known) has recently been carefully restored by Munkenbeck & Marshall.

The high tide of pre-war modernism dragged in some unlikely converts – like Marshall Sisson, an architect entranced by Fascism, whose post-1945 practice focussed on the repair of historic buildings. Harry Weedon, who designed the Villa Marina at Llandudno, North Wales, was best known as the architect of numerous Odeon cinemas in the Deco modernistic manner. The designers of modern houses were a broad school, and fervent commitment to the cause of modernism was by no means universal. One unifying factor was gender: women were still a tiny minority in the architectural profession. Elizabeth Benjamin, architect of East Wall at Hedgerley, Buckinghamshire, had, surprisingly perhaps, worked in Lutyens' office before setting up her own office. East Wall, her most important work, was designed in collaboration with Godfrey Samuel, sometime of Tecton. A strongly political figure, Benjamin admired the social agenda of Lubetkin – one of her clients was the Labour politician, Dr Edith Summerskill – and saw her private houses as test-beds for the social architecture of the future.

Crittall's Silver End, alas, remained a rare Pre-War example of a Modern Movement settlement for "the masses" (though the 1930s saw the first examples of modernist high-density housing, including the Quarry Hill estate in Leeds and the Kensal House project led by Max Fry, while the Bata shoe company built housing as part of a consistently modernist factory settlement at East Tilbury in Essex). Modern (or, more commonly, modernistic) suburban developments were aimed at a prosperous middle class clientele. Frinton Park, at Frinton-on-Sea, Essex, was planned to contain 1200 houses, plus public buildings. Oliver Hill was appointed architect in charge in 1934. According to historian Jill Lever, Frinton was seen as "the Le Touquet or Deauville of Essex." Relatively little was actually built: most of the area was developed after 1945 in a dismal bungaloid manner. Yet Frinton contains the largest concentration of modern houses in Britain, some of them by Hill, others by his collaborators, who included the locally based Page & Shelton as well as Howard Robertson, Frederick Etchells, and Marshall Sisson. Significantly, hard-core modernists like Lubetkin, Yorke and Wells Coates declined to work at Frinton since they were unable to accept the regime of conventional construction (rendered brick, not concrete) imposed by the developers.

Lubetkin's group of eight houses at Haywards Heath, Sussex, was designed for a client who, prefiguring the efforts of Span in the 1950s and 60s, wanted to build modern spec houses to compete with the dismal products of the typical house builder and challenged Lubetkin to produce a scheme. These unassuming houses were conventionally planned and faced in brick – curved concrete porches are a concession to Tecton's expressive leanings. When the designs were submitted to Cuckfield Urban District Council, they were turned down and the matter went to a hard-fought planning appeal. The "Cuckfield Case" ended in victory for Tecton and its client, Mr Barnett and the houses were built.

More modest was the project designed by Mary Crowley (later a leading designer of Post-War Hertfordshire schools) and Cecil Kemp at Tewin, Hertfordshire. One of the three houses was for Crowley's parents, another for Kemp himself and the third for some close friends. Constructed of local brick, the houses featured a pioneering monopitch roof, a response to the problems which had already arisen with flat roofs, and look forward to the pragmatic and humane housing seen in the Post-War new towns.

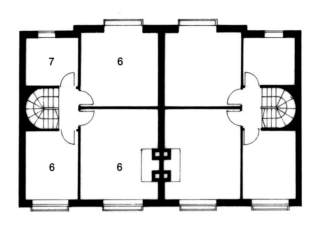

First Floor Plan Type 'A'

Lubetkin & Tecton
Sunnywood Road
Haywards Heath
West Sussex
1934-36

1 Entrance
2 Kitchen
3 Dining recess
4 Living room
5 Balcony
6 Bedroom
7 Bathroom
8 WC

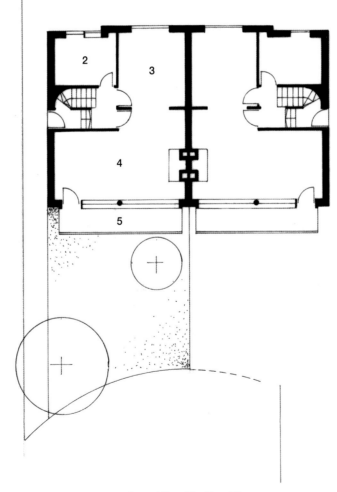

Ground Floor Plan Type 'A'

0 1   10

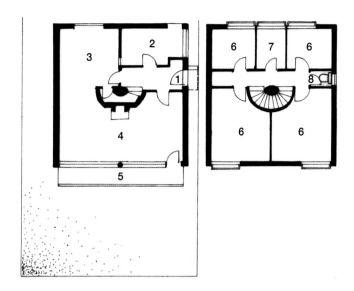

Ground Floor Plan / First Floor Plan Type 'C'

Ground Floor Plan / First Floor Plan Type 'B'

This development of eight modest houses by Tecton hints at the way in which modernism could have infiltrated the spec building industry – given a greater commitment by developers and without the disaster of the Second World War. After the War, Tecton built on a big scale, but for public authorities.

Orchard Road   Mary B Crowley   1935-36
Tewin, Hertfordshire   & Cecil G Kemp

new suburban forms

The three houses at Orchard Road, Tewin, Hertfordshire, were built for related families – one was for architect Mary Crowley's parents, another for her collaborator, Cecil Kemp. These houses were allegedly the first in Britain to adopt the Scandinavian device of a monopitch roof. The houses are built of modest local brick, a far remove from the all-white image of the modern house.

The Round House   Oliver Hill   Mid-1930s
Frinton-on-Sea, Essex

new suburban forms

This circular house by Oliver Hill was originally built as a sales kiosk for the new township, intended as a modernist experiment, but later abandoned to conventional suburban development.

St Martin
Frinton-on-Sea, Essex

Oliver Hill

Mid-1930s

At Frinton-on-Sea a modernist seaside town was planned with Oliver Hill as architect in charge. In 1935, after a year in post, Hill resigned, in protest against what he saw as timidity and compromise on the part of the client. Only a limited number of modern houses were built – after 1945, development continued in a banal "traditional" manner.

new suburban forms

14 – 16 Waltham Way   Architect Unknown   Mid-1930s
Frinton-on-Sea, Essex

More typical of Frinton are these stylish, but generally conventional, houses in the modernistic manner.

Dawn   Oliver Hill   Mid-1930s
Frinton-on-Sea, Essex

Oliver Hill's work at Frinton involved the use of a series of standard motifs, including the use of large, curved windows. At Dawn on Quendon Way, one of the first houses built, many original features remain. Morae on Easton Way was more elaborate and expensive than the typical Frinton house.

Morare   Oliver Hill   Mid-1930s

Frinton-on-Sea, Essex

Lytton Close   G G Winbourne   Mid-1930s
Hampstead Garden Suburb,
London

Lytton Close is an extraordinary sight: a modernistic intrusion into the generally brick Tudor confines of
Hampstead Garden Suburb. The symmetry and Deco detailing of these elegant houses is typical of
developers' modernistic around Britain – but, unusually, these houses are well maintained and little altered.

looking forward: the end of the modern house?

The outbreak of war in September, 1939, put an effective end to private house building for more than a decade. When the rebuilding of Britain began in the early 50s, modernist pioneers like Yorke, Lubetkin, Denys Lasdun, Leslie Martin, Max Fry and his wife Jane Drew and Ernö Goldfinger took the lead as the designers of public buildings, schools, universities and housing estates, along with architects of a younger generation like Powell & Moya and Chamberlin, Powell & Bon. Peter Moro, a refugee from Hitler, whose Harbour Meadow at Birdham, West Sussex (designed with Richard Llewelyn-Davies) was perhaps the last modern house to be completed before the War, won new distinction with his fine interiors for the Festival Hall. A new generation of modern houses, designed by architects such as Colin St John Wilson, Patrick Gwynne (whose Homewood at Esher remains one of the finest Pre-War houses), James Stirling, Peter Aldington, John Winter, Michael Manser and the young Rogers and Foster reflected new influences, not least that of the United States' West Coast.

Had the War not arbitrarily ended the saga of the modern house, would the experimentation and sheer bolshie bravado of the 1930s have matured into a way of building with the potential to become, as F R S Yorke, envisaged "the normal architecture of the country?" The English Arts and Crafts and neo-Georgian traditions were far from dead (as the successful Post-War careers of architects like Donald McMorran, Francis Johnson and Raymond Erith confirm) and the spec housing market remained overwhelmingly traditional in its inclinations. Yet by 1939 the architecture of modernism was already assuming a striking maturity, coming to terms with the culture of the land. In fact, the image of the modern house as an all-white (or pink) box, a half-digested rehash of the Villa Savoye, is at best a gross generalisation. Maxwell Fry's Little Winch was the outcome of yet another planning battle. Architect and client wanted a flatroofed house of exposed concrete. The local council demanded a pitched roof. Eventually a flat roof was permitted, on the condition that the house be faced in "traditional" materials – brick and weather boarding were applied in an odd premonition of Fry's mature style. At Bentley Wood, Halland, Sussex, completed in 1938, Chermayeff used timber construction and clad the walls in cedar boarding. Few modern houses of the era have a more felicitous relationship with the English landscape. Yorke & Breuer were content to use stock brick for their houses at Eton – a commission from the college. At Brackenfell in Cumbria, Leslie Martin and his wife Sadie Speight responded to the context by using local stone as a cladding material. An extreme example of deference to place and history can be found in Raymond McGrath's Carrygate (formerly Land's End) at Galby, Leicestershire, where the ground floor was clad in recycled bricks from a demolished Elizabethan house. With its timber-clad upper floor, the house was a far remove from the purity of St Ann's Hill.

Ernö Goldfinger, the Hungarian-born pupil of Perret whose earliest executed works in Britain were shop interiors, was lambasted by some local residents for his proposed demolition of a modest group of cottages close to Hampstead Heath. The cottages were, however, demolished and in 1938 Goldfinger's Willow Road houses rose in their place. At Willow Road, Ernö and Ursula Goldfinger spent the rest of their lives, so that the house became a rich collage of furnishings, works of art and personal effects. The furore over its construction notwithstanding – local author Ian Fleming allegedly named his worst villain after Goldfinger – the "terrace" at Willow Road seemed to draw some inspiration from that tradition of well-mannered, liveable urban architecture celebrated by Steen Eiler Rasmussen in *London: The Unique City* (1934). The order and rationality of Georgian urban building, indeed, appealed to modernists – John Summerson, the greatest historian of Georgian architecture, was a firm adherent of the Modern Movement.

The acquisition of 2 Willow Road by the National Trust seemed to be the meeting point of two histories, that of a campaigning, Arts and Crafts-rooted tradition, concerned with landscape, history and identity and another radical tradition (for such it had become) with its origins in 1900s Vienna and 1920s Paris concerned to use architecture and design to remake society. With the acquisition of Patrick Gwynne's The Homewood, the Trust has become a committed defender of the Modern Movement.

The continuing listing programme of English Heritage and the campaigning activities of the Twentieth Century (formerly Thirties) Society have extended the umbrella of protection to a high proportion of surviving modern houses. But the best form of protection for any building is ownership by someone who appreciates its qualities and is determined to protect them. Too many 1930s modern (and modernistic) houses have been spoiled by crude extensions, external refacing, internal remodelling and the replacement of original windows and doors with cheap substitutes. It seems extraordinary that, as recently as 1984, Yorke's Torilla at Hatfield was delisted at the request of its then owner. The house was allowed to fall into near-ruin and in 1993 a public inquiry was held into proposals to demolish it and redevelop the site. Fortunately, by then, reason had prevailed. The house was listed II* and the demolition proposals were rejected. Now Torilla has an owner who loves it and, after restoration by John Winter, it looks splendid and is a hugely enjoyable place to live. From being an oddity and an apparent anomaly in conservative Britain, the modern house has become part of the "heritage", a treasured asset. It still has the power to inspire and even to shock and is now informing the work of a new generation of architects born long after the last of the great modern houses was completed.

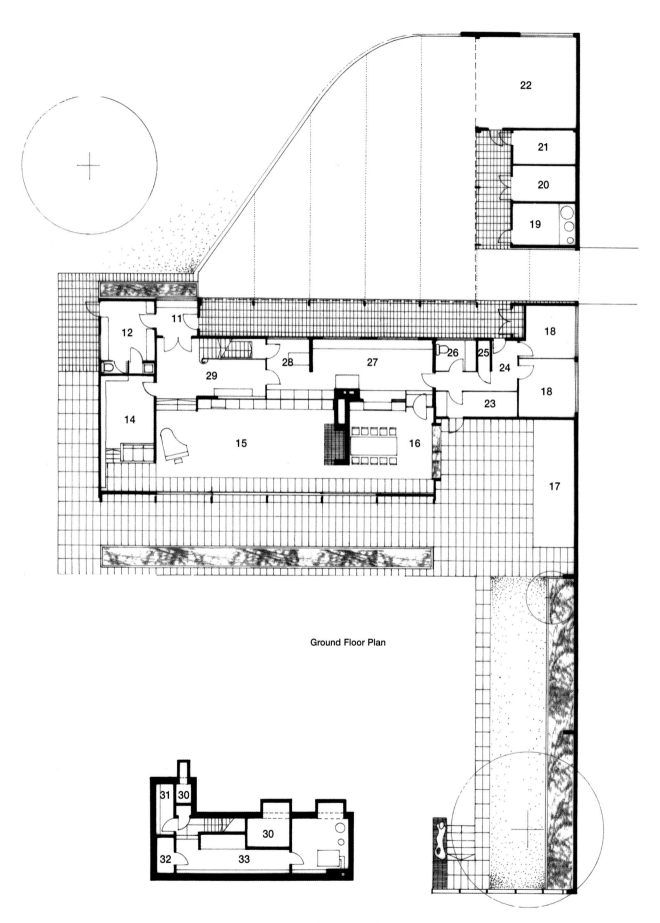

Ground Floor Plan

Basement Plan

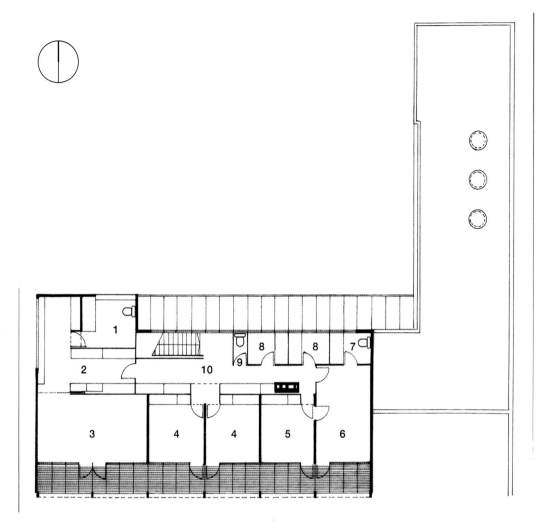

First Floor Plan

Chermayeff
Bentley Wood
Halland
East Sussex
1935-38

1   Bathroom
2   Dressing room
3   Master bedroom
4   Guest room
5   Night nursery
6   Day nursery
7   Nursery bathroom
8   Guest bathroom
9   WC
10 Stair hall
11 Vestibule
12 Cloakroom
13 Shower
14 Study
15 Living room
16 Dining room
17 Pool
18 Servant's rooms
19 Water purification plant
20 Garden store
21 Laundry
22 Garage
23 Terrace store
24 Service entrance
25 Larder
26 Servant's bathroom
27 Kitchen
28 Servant's sitting space
29 Hall
30 Fuel store
31 Wine cellar
32 Trunk store
33 Corridor

0   1   10

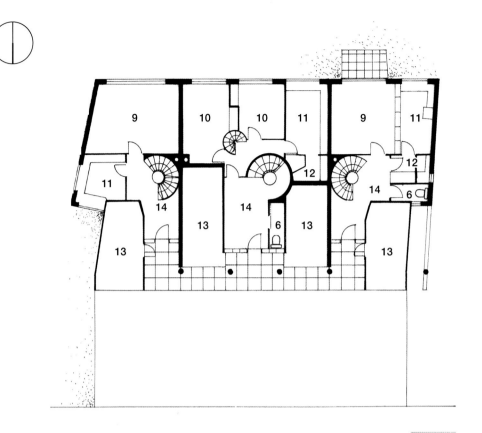

Ernö Goldfinger
Willow Road
Hampstead
London
1937-39

1 Garden room
2 Laundry
3 Nursery
4 Boilers
5 Box room
6 WC
7 Workshop
8 Fuel store
9 Dining room
10 Maid's bedroom
11 Kitchen
12 Larder
13 Garage
14 Hall
15 Living room
16 Bedroom
17 Studio
18 Study
19 Wardrobe
20 Bathroom

Ground Floor Plan

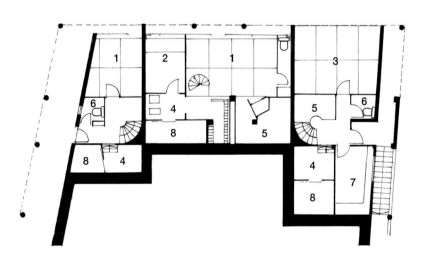

Basement Plan

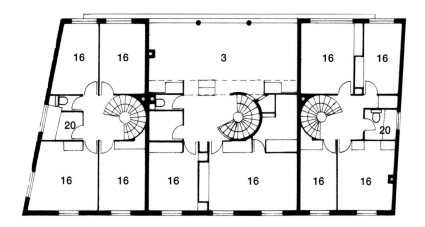

Second Floor Plan

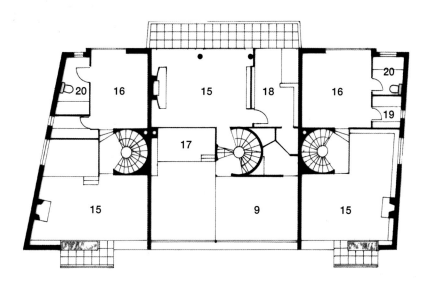

First Floor Plan

0 1   10

Bentley Wood   Serge Chermayeff   1935-38
Halland, East Sussex

looking forward: the end of the modern house?

Chermayeff's Bentley Wood, completed in 1938, suggests the degree to which modern architecture was achieving a new maturity in the years before the War. The use of a timber frame and cedar cladding shows the architect's concern for context.

In its matter of factness and common sense, Bentley Wood looks forward to the (non-domestic) modernism of the Post-War years, the style of the Hertfordshire schools and New Towns.

Little Winch   E Maxwell Fry   1934
Chipperfield, Hertfordshire

looking forward: the end of the modern house?

Even the erstwhile hardliners Connell, Ward & Lucas were prepared to move in a more naturalistic and contextual direction in this house of 1938.

Two houses for Eton masters were commissioned by the College from Yorke & Breuer in 1937-38. Faced in brick, undemonstrative but with an almost Georgian urbanity, these houses remain in their original use.

Benson House   Yorke & Breuer   1937-38
Eton, Berkshire

The Wood House   Gropius & Fry   1937

Shipbourne, Kent

The contrast between this house of 1937 and earlier houses by Gropius and Fry is marked – here there is no attempt to impose an aesthetic which might seem at odds with the local terrain.

Carry Gate   Raymond McGrath   1937-39
Galby, Leicestershire

looking forward: the end of the modern house?

Raymond McGrath's Land's End (as it was originally named) was completed in 1939 and makes good use of timber cladding – in response to opposition from locals to the original choice of materials.

Brackenfell   J L Martin & Sadie Speight   1937-38
Brampton, Cumbria

Brackenfell is another unequivocally modern, yet contextual, house, in this instance located in deepest Cumbria. The architect was Leslie Martin, working with his wife Sadie Speight. Martin was later to head the LCC's architects' department and, as head of the architecture school at Cambridge, to impose his manner on several generations of practitioners. He died in 2000.

Willow Road   Ernö Goldfinger   1937-39
Hampstead, London

Ernö Goldfinger's terrace of houses overlooking Hampstead Heath was widely disliked when first built – the author Ian Fleming was a strident objector to the project. The centre house, where Goldfinger and his family lived, is now the property of the National Trust, part of "the heritage", an outcome which Goldfinger would have found pleasing but possibly surprising.

looking forward: the end of the modern house?

Nick Dawe would like to acknowledge the generosity and kindness of the owners of houses featured within this book, which he dedicates to his wife Caroline.

Kenneth Powell wishes to acknowledge the inspiration of the Twentieth Century Society, whose tours and publications have done so much to rekindle interest in the Modern House.

Nick Dawe would like to acknowledge the financial assistance of the following, without whose support this publication would not have been possible: Lord Palumbo, Metro Imaging, Mike Davies, John Deverall and Fujifilm.

The publisher would like to thank the following for their comment towards the development of this publication: Mark Dorrian, Eric Parry, Alan Powers, Kevin Rhowbotham and the Twentieth Century Society.

The line work in The Modern House Today is based on original drawings published in the 1930s and 40s. The research and re-drawing of this material was done by James B Taylor.

© 2001 Black Dog Publishing Limited, Nick Dawe and Kenneth Powell

Edited and produced by Duncan McCorquodale

Designed by mono / www.monosite.co.uk

Printed in the European Union

■■■

Architecture Art Design Fashion History Photography Theory and Things

Black Dog Publishing Limited

5 Ravenscroft Street

London

E2 7SH

UK

T 44 020 7613 1922

F 44 020 7613 1944

E info@bdp.demon.co.uk

ISBN: 1 901033 72 4